Original pictorial title. An offering of plants is being made to Rerum Magistra (the Mistress, or Teacher, of Nature). In the sky Apollo and Aquarius represent the sun and rain needed by plants.

DECORATIVE FLORAL ENGRAVINGS

118 plates from the 1696
"Accurate Description of Terrestrial Plants"
by
ABRAHAM MUNTING

Edited by
Theodore Menten

Dover Publications, Inc., New York

Published in Canada by General Publishing Company, Ltd., 30 Lesmill Road, Don Mills, Toronto,
Ontario.
Published in the United Kingdom by Constable
and Company, Ltd., 10 Orange Street, London WC 2.

*Decorative Floral Engravings: 118 Plates from the
1696 "Accurate Description of Terrestrial Plants"*
is a new selection of plates from *Naauwkeurige
Beschryving der Aardgewassen*, originally published
in 1696 by Pieter vander Aa in Leyden and François
Halma in Utrecht. (See the new Publisher's Note
for the full original title and further bibliographic
data.)

DOVER *Pictorial Archive* SERIES

International Standard Book Number: 0-486-23117-8
Library of Congress Catalog Card Number: 74-83764

Manufactured in the United States of America
Dover Publications, Inc.
180 Varick Street
New York, N. Y. 10014

Illustration on original typographic title page. Minerva and Ceres view a picture of harvesters. The Latin motto reads: "Life is more elegant for them (or, through these things)."

Publisher's Note

The seventeenth century in Holland was a golden age of gardening and of botanical illustration. One of the most beautiful books of this period was the work of Abraham Munting, who taught the then allied sciences of medicine and botany at the Academy of Groningen, where he also superintended a noteworthy botanical garden nicknamed "Groningen's Paradise."

In this era of intensive exploration and active scientific interchange of plants among world scholars, Munting kept abreast of all botanical discoveries and developments. He was interested not only in classification but also in the uses (especially medicinal) of plants and in the best methods of growing them successfully for pleasure and use as well. He published a book called *Ware Oeffening der Planten* (True Plant Practice) in 1672, and reprinted it in 1682. But his information and experience kept accumulating, and by the 1690s he was ready to bring out a book three times as long—and illustrated with many elegant copperplates.

Munting died while his *magnum opus* was in the press; his partially written "Notice to the Reader" was completed by the bookseller-publishers, Pieter vander Aa of Leyden and François Halma of Utrecht, who also wrote the dedication to the burgomasters of Leyden. The book was published in 1696 with the title:

Naauwkeurige Beschryving der Aardgewassen, Waar in de veelerley Aart en bijzondere Eigenschappen der Boomen, Heesters, Kruyden, Bloemen, Met haare Vrugten, Zaden, Wortelen en Bollen, Neevens derzelver waare Voort-teeling, gelukkige Aanwinning, en heylzaame Genees-Krachten, Na een veel-jarige Oeffening en eigen Ondervinding, In drie onderscheide Boeken, naauwkeuriglijk beschreeven worden; Door den Heer Abraham Munting, In zijn leeven, Hoogleeraar der Genees- en Kruydkunde in de vermaarde Akademie te Groeningen. Nu eerst nieuwelijks uitgegeeven, en met meer dan 250 Afbeeldingen, alle naer's leeven geteekend en konstiglijk in 't Koper gesneeden, vercierd. Met noodige Registers verrijkt.

(Accurate description of terrestrial plants, wherein the multifarious nature and special properties of trees,

Illustration for the dedication to the burgomasters of Leyden.
Narcissus, soon to become a flower, is enamored of his reflection.

shrubs, herbs, flowers, with their fruits, seeds, roots and bulbs, together with their true propagation, successful increase and healthful curative powers, based on years of practice and personal experience, have been accurately described in three separate parts by Abraham Munting, during his life professor of medicine and botany at the celebrated academy of Groningen. Now newly published and adorned with over 250 illustrations, all drawn from life and artistically engraved on copper. Enriched with the necessary indexes.

The present volume contains a selection of 118 outstanding illustrations from Munting's book. The plants, many of them grown in his own "Paradise," were drawn under his close supervision by uncredited but obviously skillful and dedicated artists; the engraving, too, is on a high technical level throughout. Variety is added by the ribbons, pedestals, boards, etc., on which the Latin designations are engraved; by the ornate pots in which some of the plants are growing; and by the delicate landscapes, many of which suggest the habitat of the plant. The species represented here include many familiar trees, shrubs, grasses and flowers of temperate zones, along with a number of tropical and subtropical plants then relatively new to Europe.

The outlook of this volume of selected illustrations is purely artistic. For various reasons, no attempt has been made to include any of the original text, to offer modern plant names, or to group the plants botanically or otherwise (except for a few immediately obvious informal groups, like the food plants—pineapple, potato, orange, quince, banana, almond, etc.—at the end).

Following the illustrations is an alphabetical list of the Latin plant names that appear on the plates.

Illustration for a long poem in the original frontmatter, Cypresse- en Lauwerkrans (Wreath of Cypress and Laurel), *in memory of Munting. The Muses and Nymphs honor the botanist.*

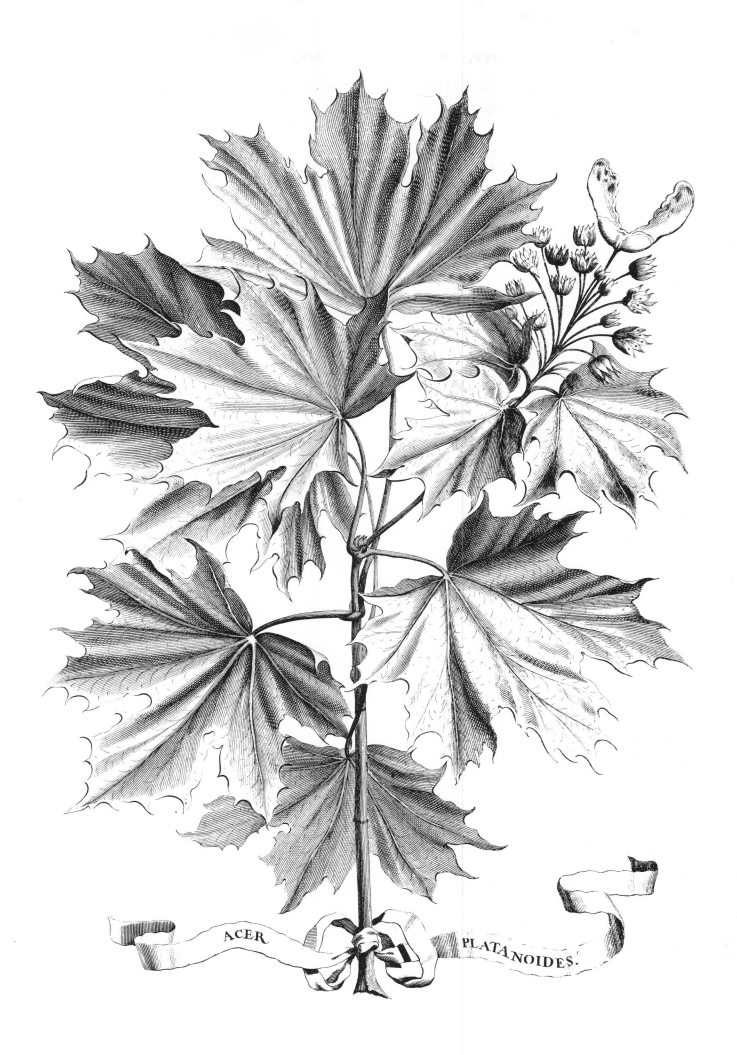

ACER PLATANOIDES.

ACACIA CORNIGERA.

ACACIA MAJOR.

SALVIA MARMOREA

SALVIA LUTEA
VARIEGATA.

PULMONARIA MACULOSA HISPIDA.

PULMONARIA MACULOSA MAXIMA.

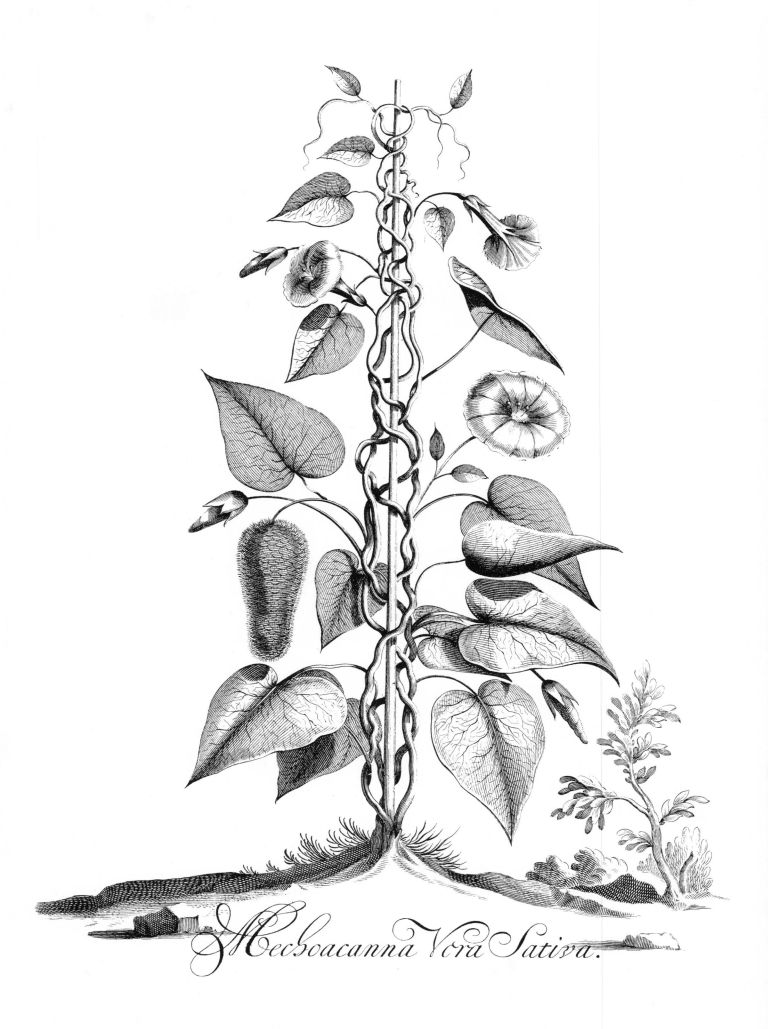

Mechoacanna Vera Sativa.

MECHOACANNA SYLVESTRIS.

I. MULDER. FECIT.

RHABARBARUM LANUGINOSUM SIVE LAPATHUM CHINENSE LONGIFOLIUM.

10

Rhabarbarum Rotundifolium Verum

11

LAPATHUM HORTENSE.

Lapathum.   Longifolium.   Crispum.

LAPATHUM UNCTUOSUM

LUTEOLA CANNABINOIDES CRETICA.

Clematis Passiflora Trifolia Flore Purpureo.

CLEMATIS PASSIFLORA PENTAPHYLLEA ANGUSTIFOLIA.

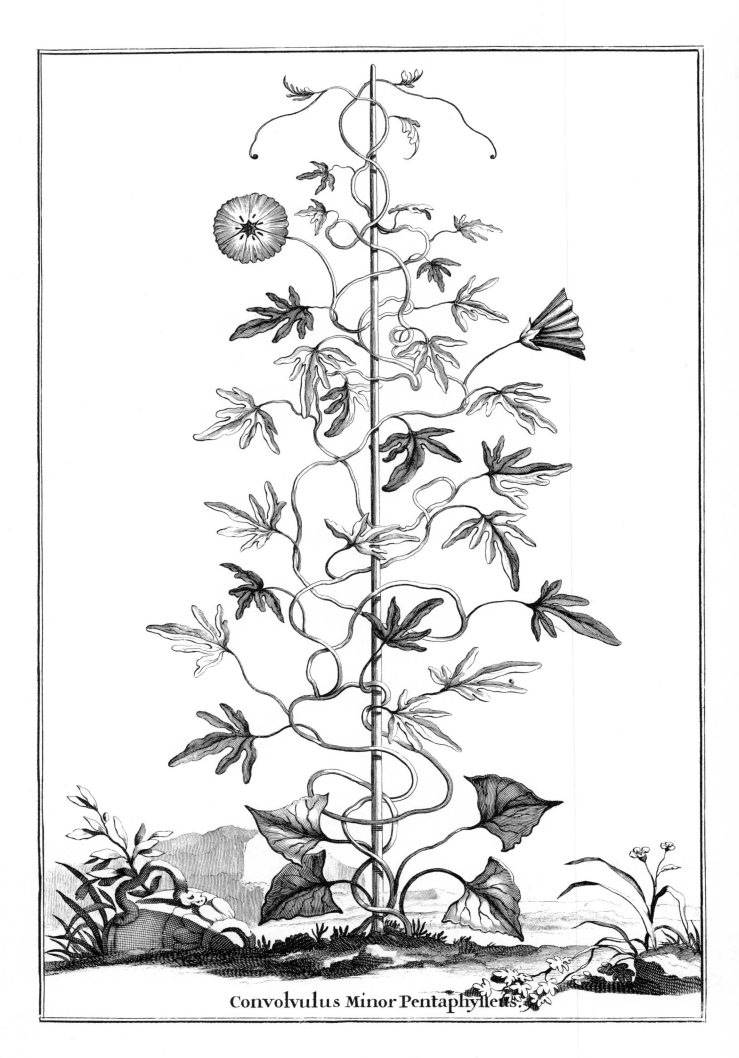

Convolvulus Minor Pentaphyllus.

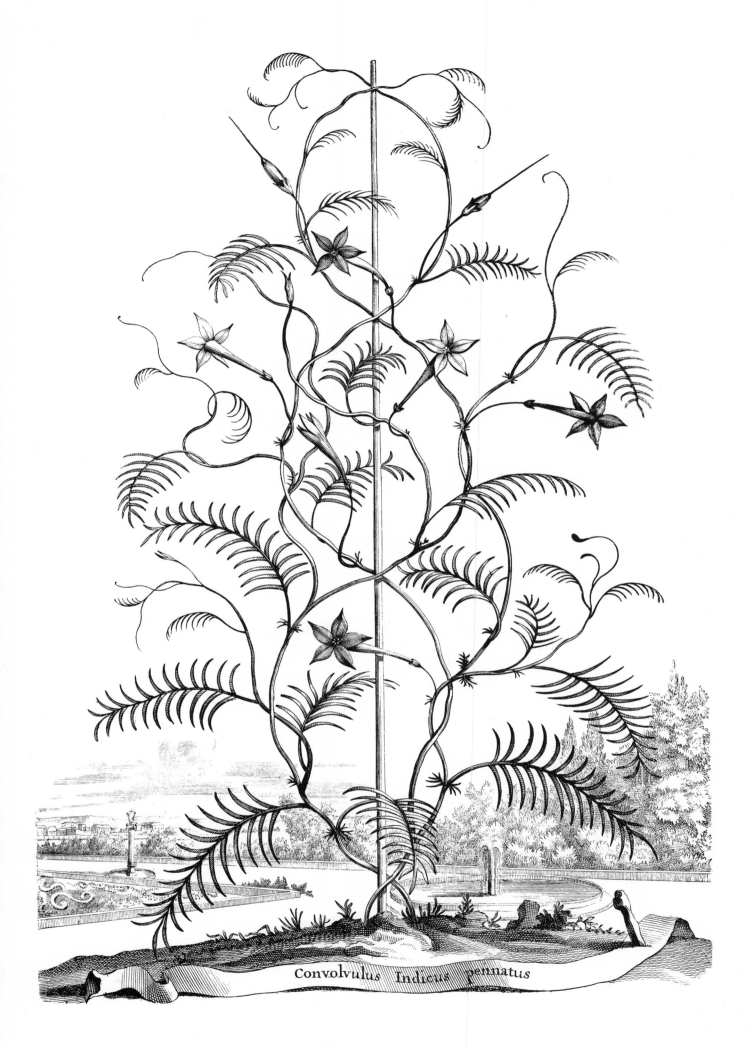

Convolvulus Indicus pennatus

19

CYCLAMEN ROTVNDIFOLIVM MAIVS AVTVMNALE.

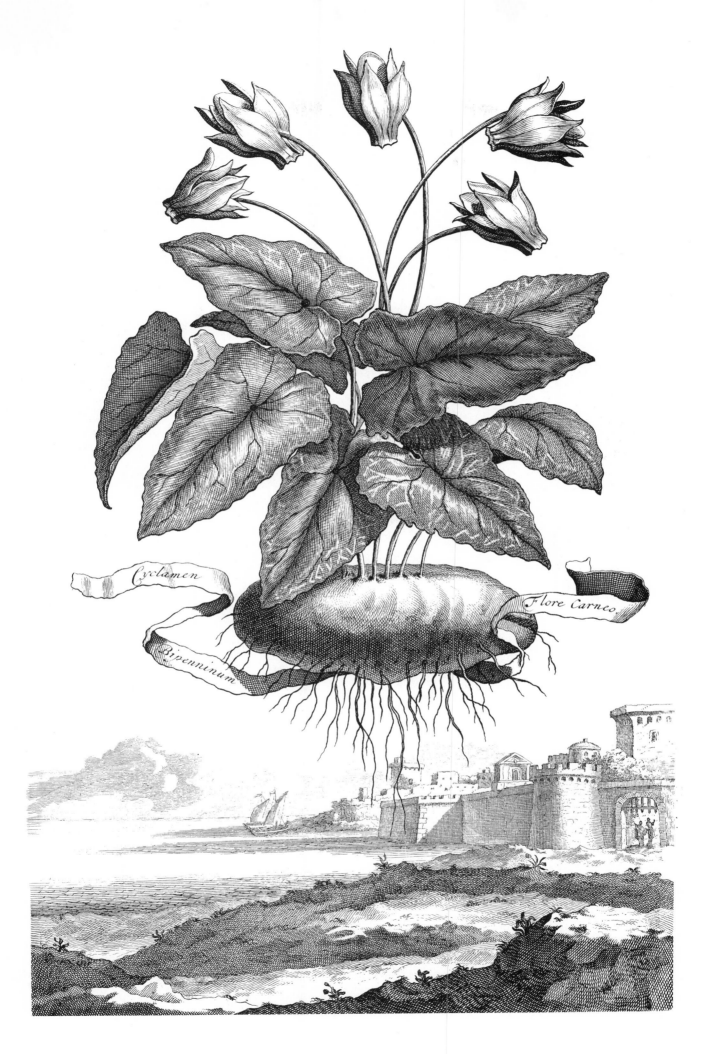

Cyclamen

Bipenninum

Flore Carneo

21

CYCLAMEN ÆSTIVUM ANEMONES
EFFIGIE RADICATUM

Cyclamen Vernum majus flore Albo odorat.

23

SEDUM CRISPUM.

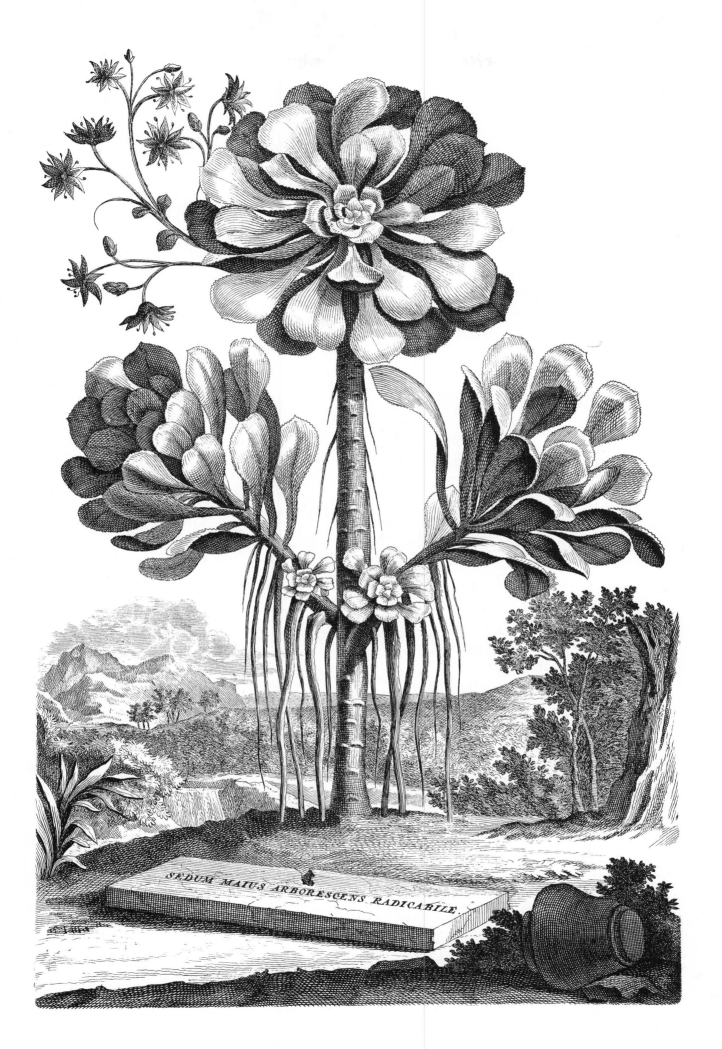

SEDUM MAIUS ARBORESCENS RADICABILE

VIOLA MARIANA ALBA PLENIFLORA

VIOLA
MATRONALIS
FLORE ALBO
ET PVRPVREO
PLENO
VARIEGATA

27

IASMINUM
PALLIDO
COERULEUM
PERSICUM
LATIFOLIUM.

28

JASMINUM SEMPER VIRENS AMERICANUM

Malva Chinensis   Rosea Arborescens

MALVA ARBORESCENS INDICA MINOR.

CISTUS MINOR ROSMARINI-FOLIUS.

CISTUS LAURIFOLIUS.

CISTUS ANNUUS SUPINUS.

34

Agrifolium non Spinosum.

AGRIFOLIUM AURATUM.

Jacea Candida Ragusiana.

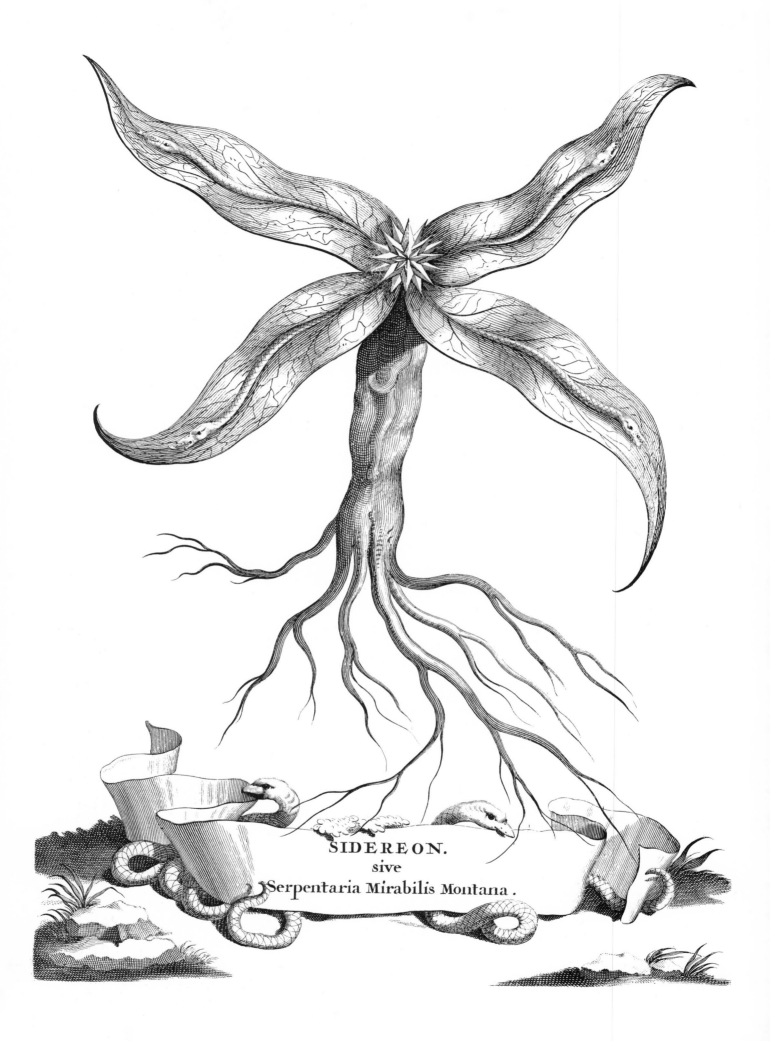

SIDEREON.
sive
Serpentaria Mirabilis Montana.

DORONICUM AMERICANUM.

MENTHASTRUM VIRGINIANUM ORIGANITES FISTULOSUM.

Aftragalus

Triangularis.

LASERPITIVM LVCIDVM.

45

Apocynum Syriacum

Latifolium Flore Glomerofo.

BORRAGO SEMPER VIRENS MAJOR

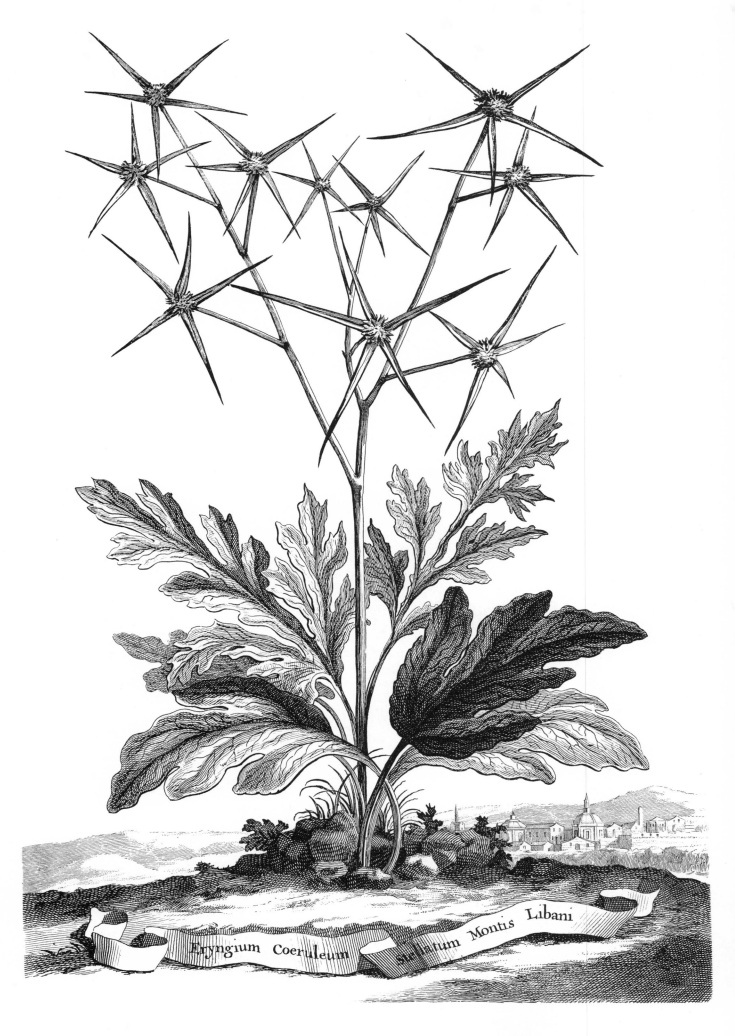

Eryngium Coeruleum stellatum Montis Libani

48

CENTAURIUM MAJUS FOLIO CINARÆ.

Chamæpitys Major Coerulea.

50

CAMPANULA   PYRAMIDALIS   MINOR.

MIRTUS LAURI-FOLIA.

MYRTUS BŒTICA PUMILA LATIFOLIA.

MYRTVS TARENTINA TENVIFOLIA MINIMA.

CHAMÆ MESPILUS ALPINA

ALCHIMILLA   PENTAPHYLLÆA.

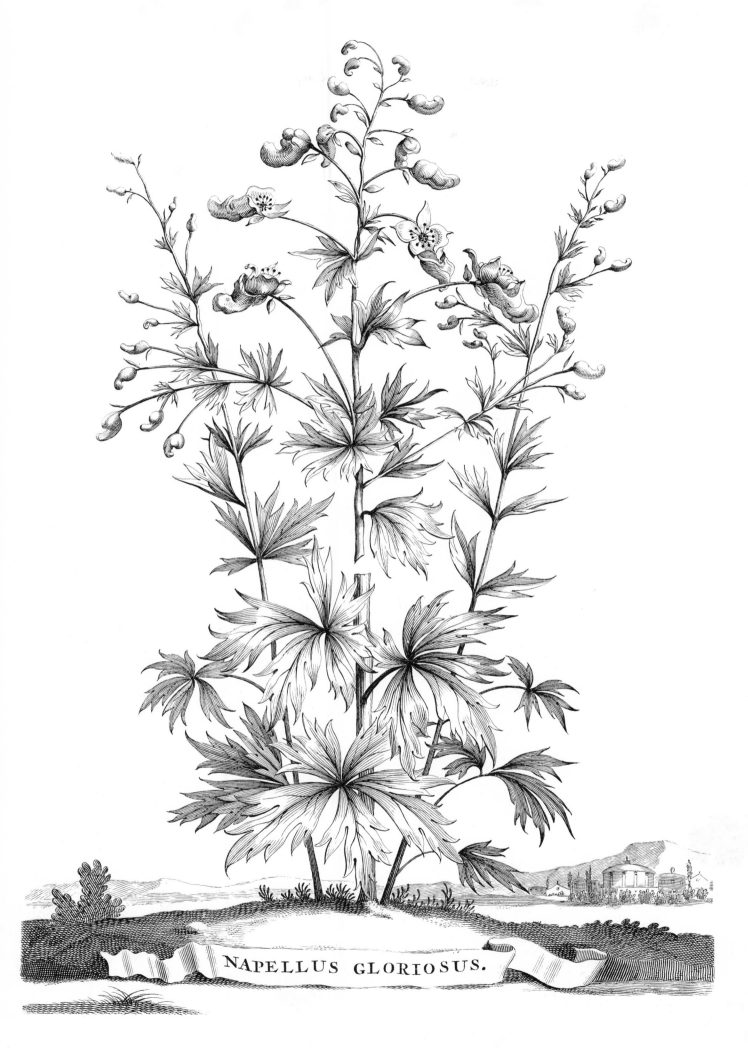

NAPELLUS GLORIOSUS.

GUAJACUM PATAVINUM MAJUS.

Sumach.   Arbor.

ABSINTHIUM LONGIFOLIUM
PENTAPHYLLEUM.

SIDERITIS

SPICATA FŒTIDA.

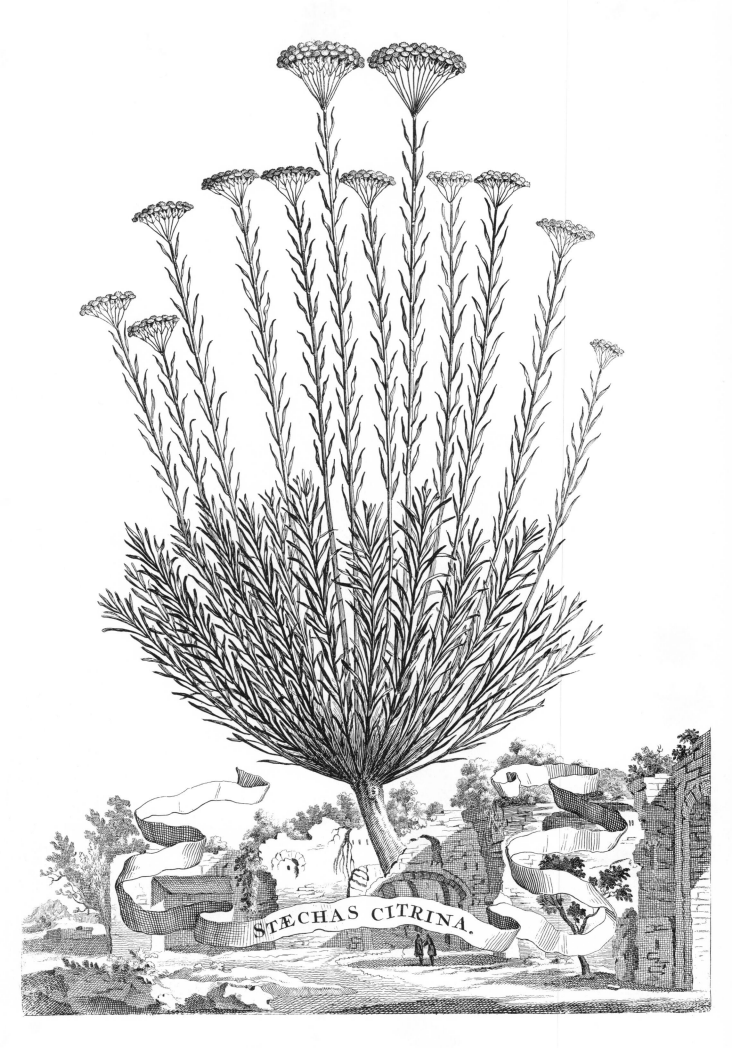

STÆCHAS CITRINA.

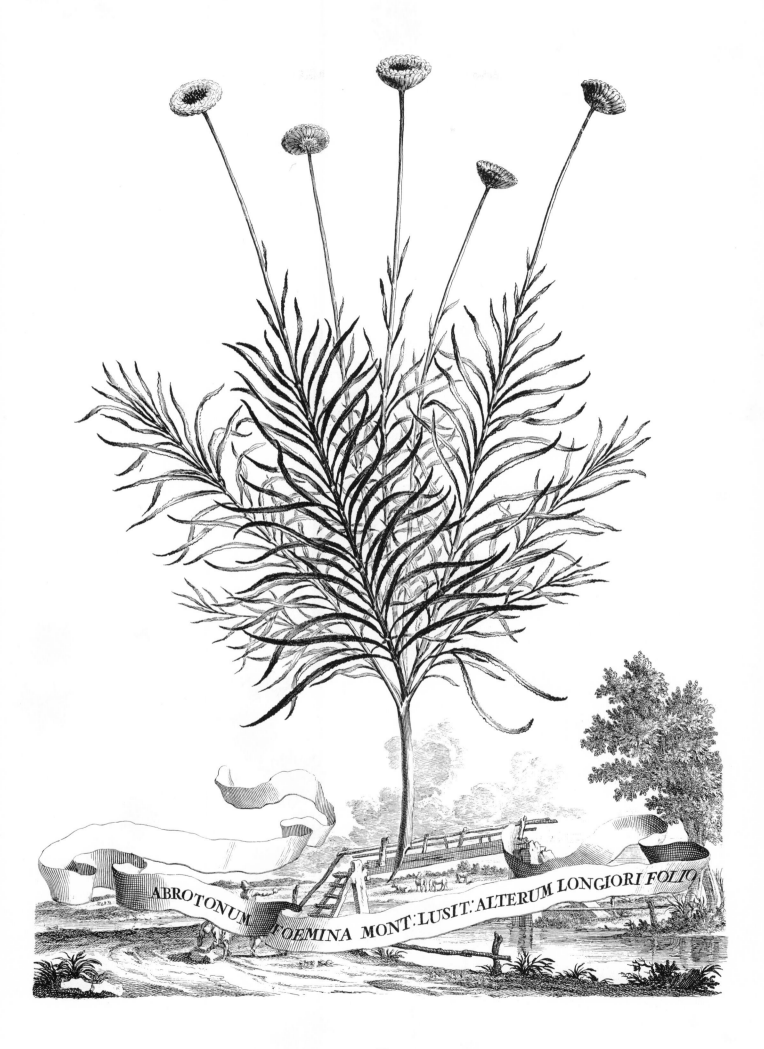

ABROTONUM FOEMINA MONT: LUSIT: ALTERUM LONGIORI FOLIO

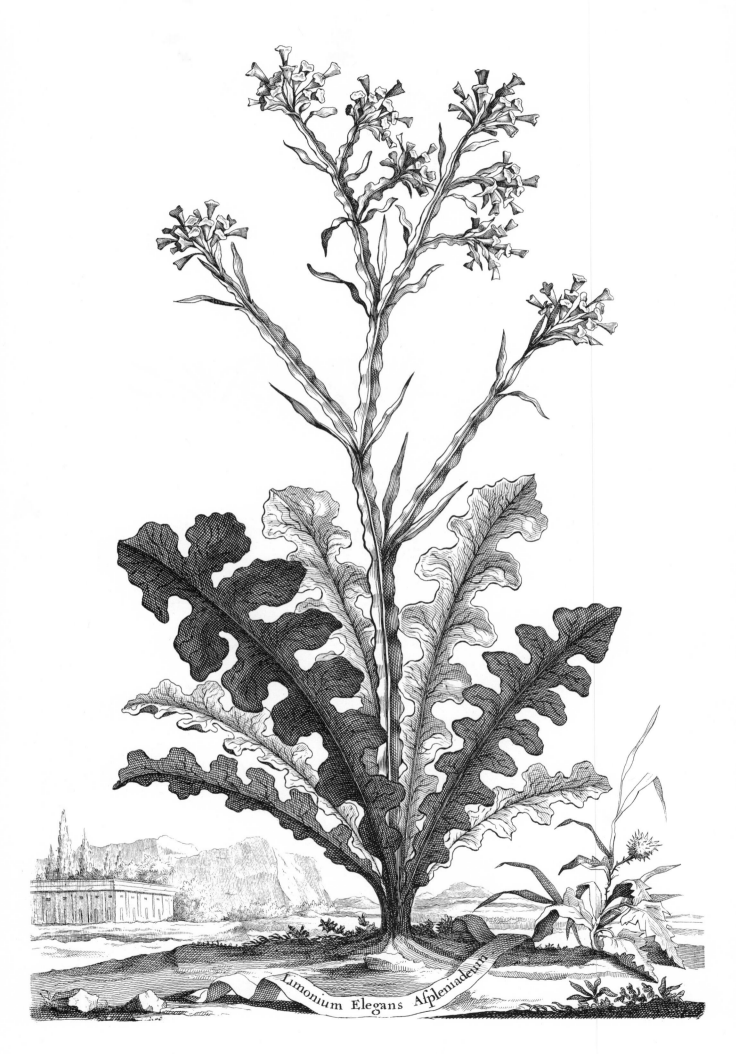

Limonium Elegans Aspleniadeum

ACETOSA HISPANICA MAXIMA.

SESAMUM PERSICUM   TRILOBATUM FOETIDUM.

Cattaria Spicata Coerulea Radice Tuberola

Seseli Æthiopicum Herba

THAPSIA MAJOR LATIFOLIA.

VALERIANELLA CAPITATA.

FILIX DENTATA.

JALAPPA MINOR PURPUREA.

Flos Africanus flore pleno Fistuloso.

Polypodium Sensibile.

74

Bellis Spinosa Cretica.

GERANIUM MALVATICUM ODORATUM INDICUM

MELISSA LÆVIS MOLUCANA.

SASSAFRAS ARBOR FOLIO FICULNEO.

ALCEA VESICARIA ÆTHIOPICA.

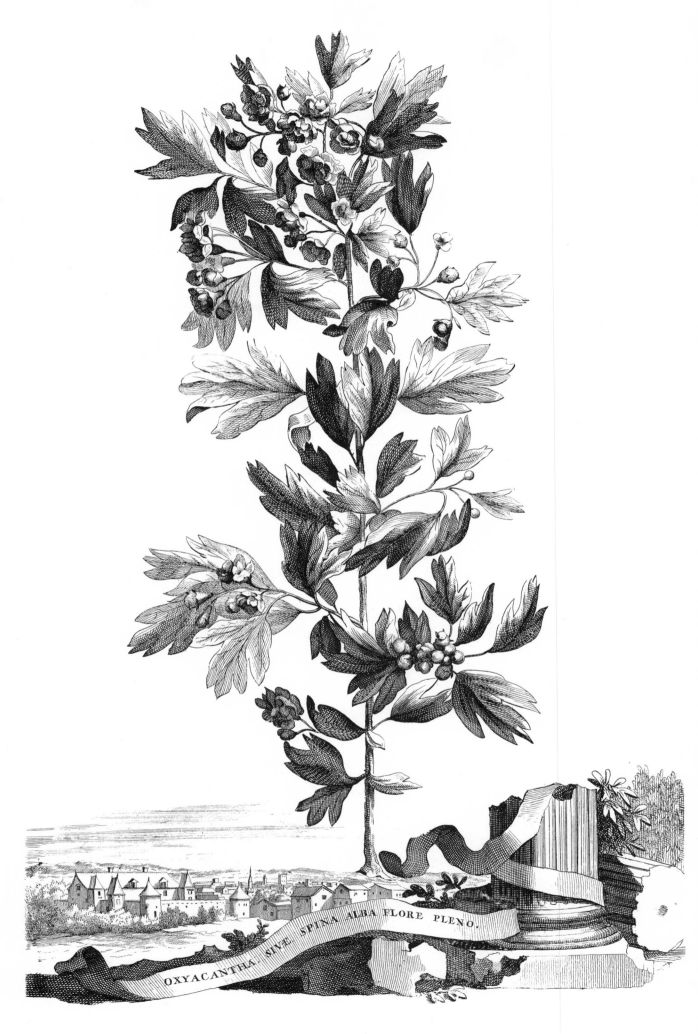

OXYACANTHA SIVE SPINA ALBA FLORE PLENO.

MYRTOPETALON·

PALMARJA.

PHALANGIUM VIRGINIANUM.

Gramen Plumeum

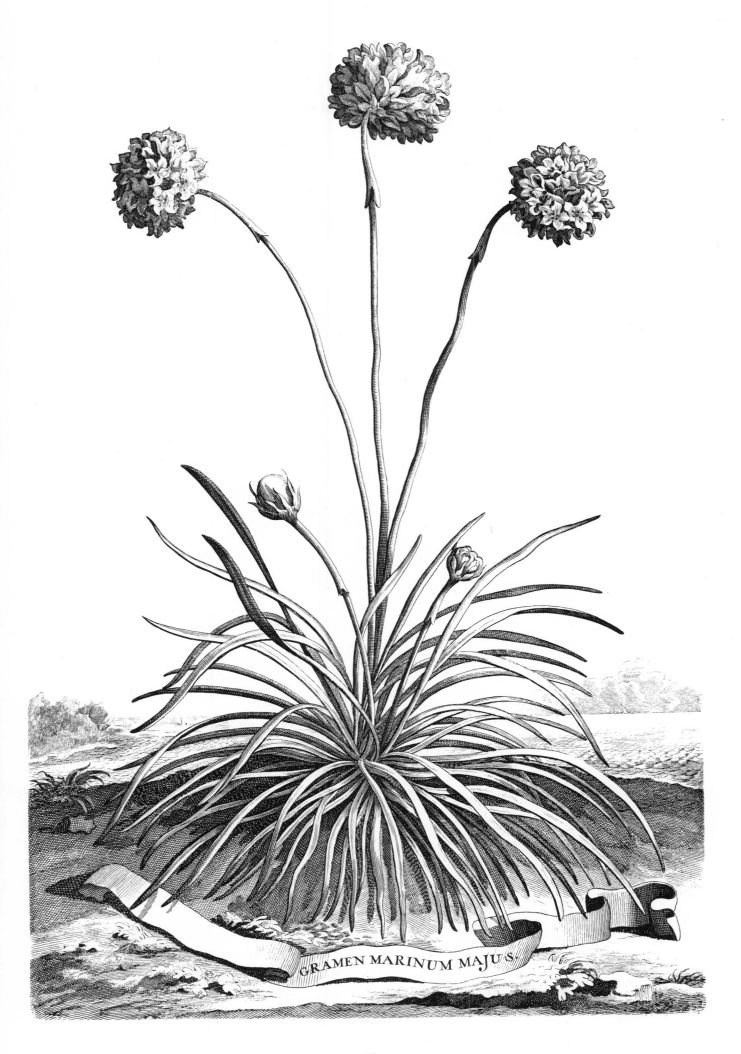

GRAMEN MARINUM MAJUS.

ARVNDO SACCHARIFERA.

86

ARVNDO AMERICANA STRIATA .

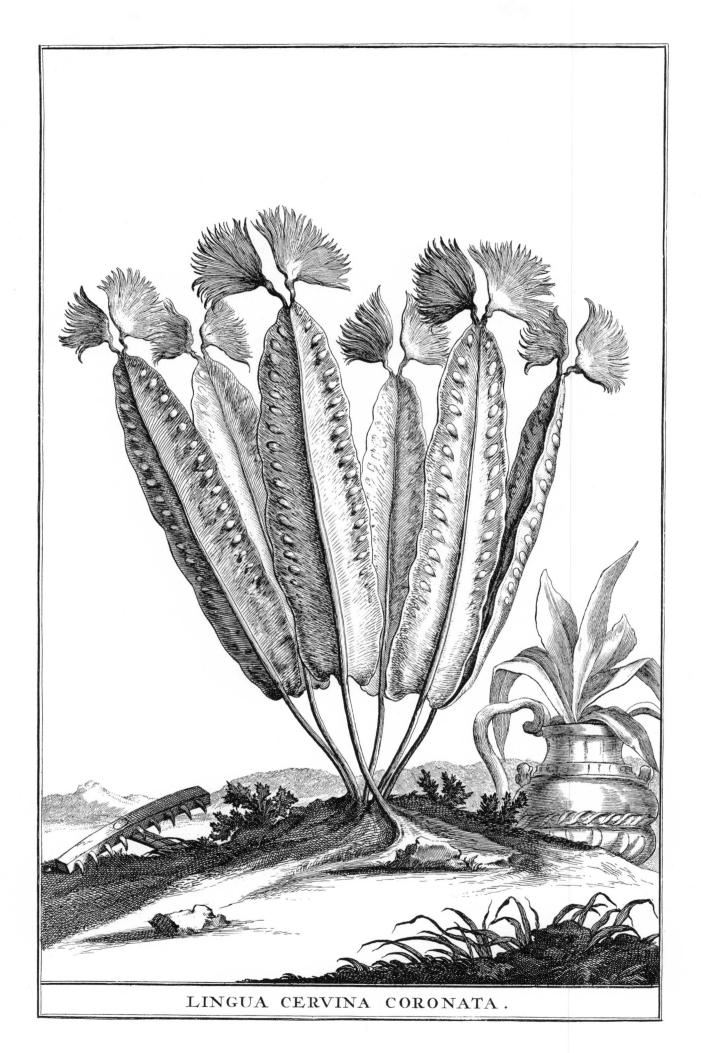

LINGUA CERVINA CORONATA.

Struthiofera.

HEMIONITIS CRISPA MAJOR.

90

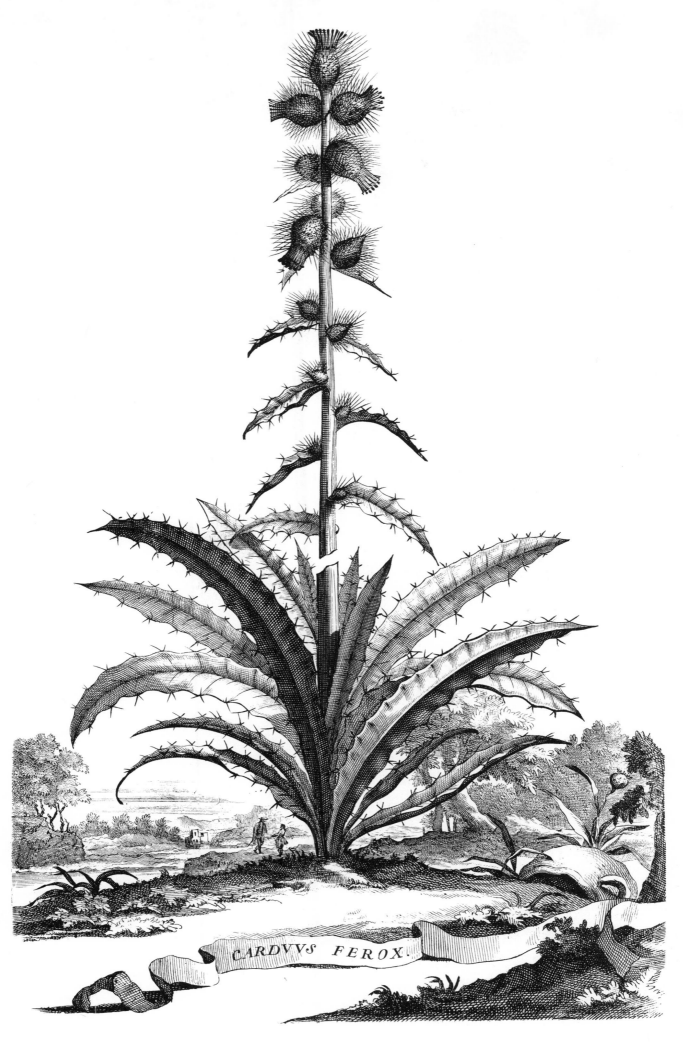

CARDVVS FEROX.

OPUNTIA MAIOR
ANGUSTIFOLIA.

ALOË MUCRONATO FOLIO
AMERICANA MAIOR.

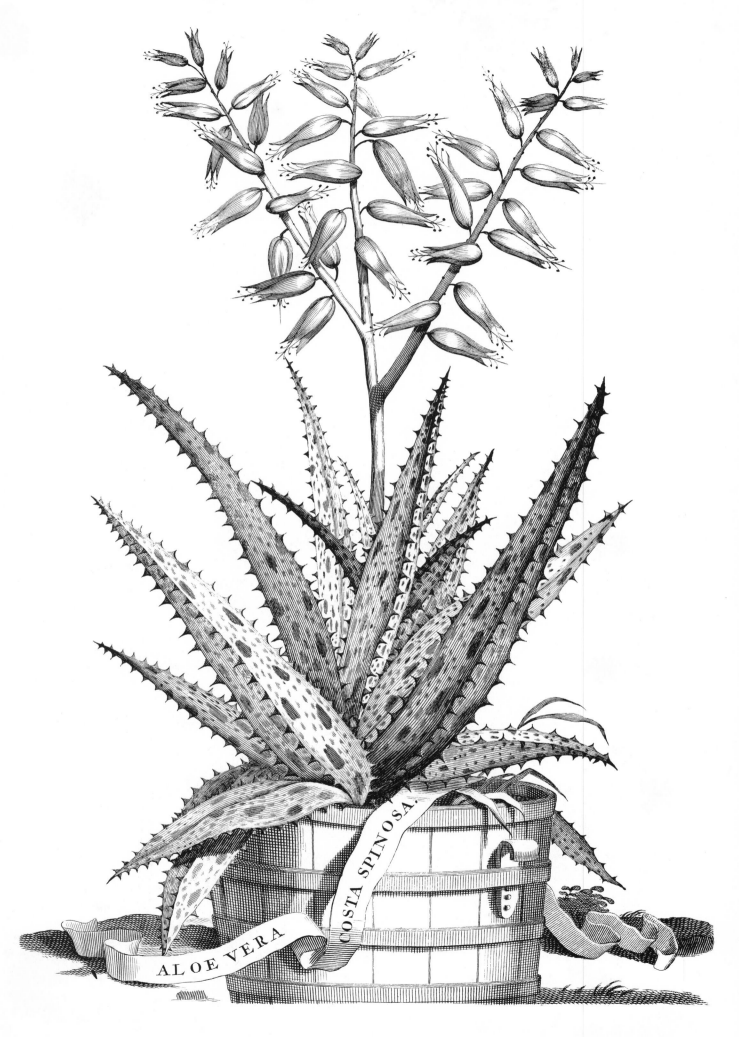

ALOE VERA

COSTA SPINOSA.

Vita Hominis plus Aloës quam Mellis habet

ALOË VERA VULGARIS.

Aloe Purpurea Lævis

96

Aloë Serrata major umbellifera

ALOË AMERICANA MINOR

PORTULACA ÆTHIOPICA.

Leontopetalon Capitatum.   Americanum.

ANANAS

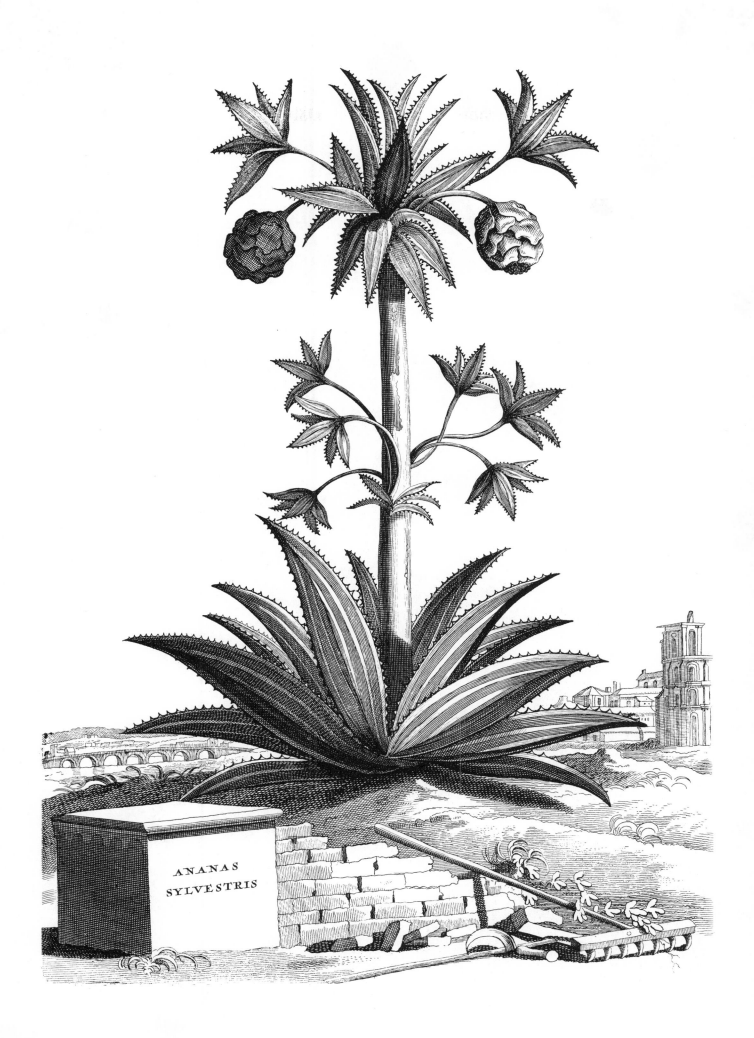

ANANAS
SYLVESTRIS

GLANS TERRESTRIS   AMERICANA.

Batata purgativæ

MALUS AURANTIA STRIIS AUREIS DISTINCTA.

106

Vitis Canadensis.

Vitis Virginiana Folis Laciniatis

Cardamomum Arborescens minus

110

CARDAMOMVM MAJVS ARBORESCENS.

MALUS CYDONIA FRUCTU CORNUTO.

Musa Fructus

Ricinus Americanus Major Rubicundus

AMYGDALVS
NANA.

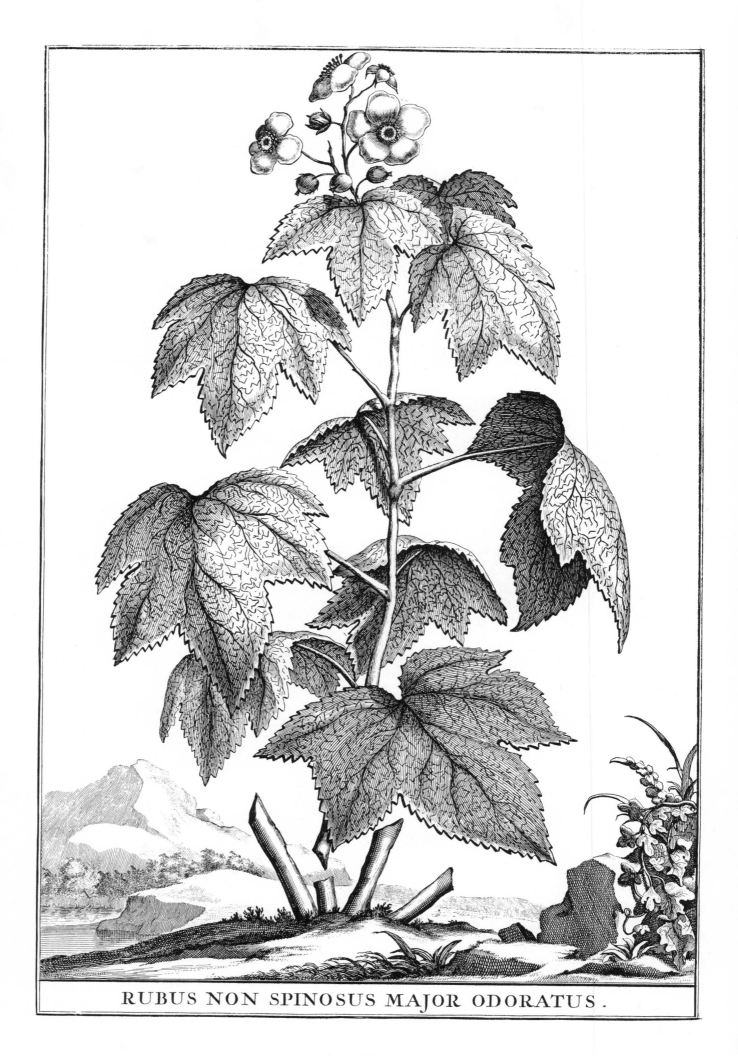

RUBUS NON SPINOSUS MAJOR ODORATUS.

SOLANUM SPINOSISSIMUM ARBORESCENS ÆTHIOPICUM.

Guanabanus Folio Ficulneo.

Alphabetical List of
Latin Plant Names